# USN AIRCRAFT 1922 - 1962

## VOL. 1

### TYPE DESIGNATION LETTER 'A', PART ONE

#### PHIL H. LISTEMANN

**NOTAM:**
This study was undertaken using the available movement cards of each USN aircraft in service between 1922 and 1962. These cards may occasionally contain errors which could lead to some disparities or omissions when the text below is compared with official or non-official publications already published.
Alphabetical order has been chosen to structure the book (except sometimes for prototype), rather than the chronological order of introduction into USN/USMC/USCG service.
Unless otherwise noted, the photographs come from the USN or from sources such as the National Archives or National Museum of Naval Aviation.

### ISBN: 978-2918590-52-1

Copyright

© 2013 Philedition - Phil Listemann

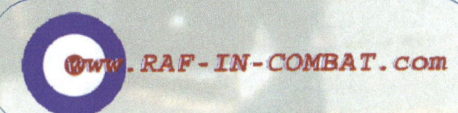

All right reserved. No part of this book may be reproduced, stored in a retrieval system or transmitted in any form by any means, electronic, mechanical, photocopying, recording or otherwise, without prior permission of the author.

Over forty years, between 1922 and 1962, the USN and USMC used a designation system which began with biplanes and ended with jets, having been used through two major wars, WW2 and the Korean War. This system remained largely the same during that time, though it evolved with the introduction of new types and technology, and new exceptions developed as well. The purpose of this series is to explain this system using photographs.

On 18 September 1962, a new system was introduced that was common to the three air arms (USAF, Army and USN/USMC) and which is still in force today. The application of this Tri-service system was effective immediately for aircraft pending delivery to the USN, but took a couple of weeks to be implemented fully in the case of aircraft already accepted, especially for aircraft based overseas or cruising on aircraft carriers.

The designation system was based on:
1 - A type designation which describes the basic mission of the aircraft.
2 - A letter designating the manufacturer (but not necessarily the designer) following the type designation.
3 - A configuration sequence indicating minor change to the aircraft type, the initial model being designated '1'.
4 - Manufacturer type sequence.
5 - Status prefix. Only two letters were assigned, **'X'** - Experimental - and **'Y'** - Service test - from 1951 onwards.
6 - Special Purpose Suffix which indicates an aircraft used in a special configuration.

**Samples:**
AD-6: Douglas First Attack type, sixth model.
F2A-1: Brewster Second Fighter type, initial model.
A3D-2P: Douglas Third Attack type, second model, reconnaissance version.
PB4Y-1: Consolidated Fourth Patrol Bomber type, initial model.

## TYPE DESIGNATION

| | | | | | |
|---|---|---|---|---|---|
| **A** | Ambulance | 1943-1946 | **P** | Pursuit | 1923 |
| | Attack | 1946-1962 | | Patrol | 1923-1962 |
| **B** | Bomber | 1931-1943 | **PB** | Patrol-Bomber | 1935-1962 |
| **BF** | Bomber-Fighter | 1934-1937 | **PTB** | Patrol, Torpedo-Bomber | 1937 |
| **BT** | Bomber-Torpedo | 1942-1945 | **R** | Racer | 1922-1928 |
| **DS** | Anti-Submarine Drone | 1959-1962 | **R** | Transport | 1931-1962 |
| **F** | Fighter | 1922-1962 | **RO** | Rotorcycle | 1954-1959 |
| **G** | Transport, Single-Engined | 1939-1941 | **S** | Anti-Submarine | 1951-1962 |
| | Inflight refuelling Tanker | 1958-1962 | **SB** | Scout-Bomber | 1934-1946 |
| **H** | Hospital | 1929-1943 | **SN** | Scout-Trainer | 1939-1962 |
| | Helicopter | 1943-1962 | **SO** | Scout-Observation | 1934-1946 |
| **J** | Transport | 1926-1931 | **T** | Torpedo | 1922-1935 |
| | General Utility | 1931-1955 | | Transport | 1927-1930 |
| **JR** | Utility Transport | 1935-1955 | | Trainer | 1948-1962 |
| **L** | Glider | 1941-1945 | **TB** | Torpedo-Bomber | 1935-1946 |
| **M** | Marine Expeditionary | 1922-1923 | **TD** | Target Drone | 1942-1946 |
| **N** | Trainer | 1922-1960 | **TS** | Torpedo-Scout | 1943 |
| **O** | Observation | 1922-1962 | **U** | Utility | 1955-1962 |
| **OS** | Observation Scout | 1935-1945 | | Unpiloted Drone | 1946-1955 |

## MANUFACTURERS CODE

| | | | | | | | | | |
|---|---|---|---|---|---|---|---|---|---|
| **A** | Aeromarine | 1922 | | Cessna | 1943 | | Gould | 1942-1945 |
| | Atlantic (Fokker) | 1927-1930 | | De Havilland Canada | 1955-1956 | | Pratt-Read | 1942-1945 |
| | General Aviation | 1930-1932 | **CH** | Caspar-Werke | 1922 | | Edo | 1943-1946 |
| | Brewster | 1935-1943 | **D** | Douglas | 1922-1962 | | Hiller | 1948-1962 |
| | Allied (Gliders only) | 1941-1943 | | McDonnell | 1942-1946 | | Cessna | 1951-1962 |
| | Noorduyn | 1946 | | Radioplane | 1943-1962 | **F** | Fokker | 1922 |
| **B** | Aerial | 1922 | | Frankfort | 1945-1946 | | Grumman | 1931-1962 |
| | Boeing | 1923-1959 | **DH** | De Havilland | 1927-1931 | | Fairchild Canada | 1942-1945 |
| | Beechcraft | 1937-1945 | **DW** | Dayton-Wright | 1922-1923 | **G** | Gallaudet | 1922 |
| | Budd | 1942-1944 | **E** | Elias | 1922-1924 | | Eberhart | 1927-1928 |
| **BS** | Blackburn | 1922 | | Detroit | 1928 | | Great Lakes | 1929-1936 |
| **C** | Curtiss | 1922-1946 | | Bellanca | 1931-1937 | | Aga Aviation | 1942 |
| | Culver | 1943-1946 | | Piper | 1941-1945 | | Goodyear | 1942-1962 |

|    |                      |           |     |                      |           |   |                  |           |
|----|----------------------|-----------|-----|----------------------|-----------|---|------------------|-----------|
|    | Globe                | 1946-1959 |     | Spartan              | 1940-1941 | W | Wright           | 1922-1926 |
| H  | Huff-Daland          | 1941-1945 |     | Piper (gliders)      | 1942-1943 |   | Waco             | 1934-1945 |
|    | Hall                 | 1928-1940 |     | Piasecki             | 1946-1962 |   | CCF              | 1942-1945 |
|    | Stearman-Hammond     | 1937-1938 | PL  | Parnall              | 1922      | X | Cox-Klemin       | 1922-1924 |
|    | Howard               | 1941-1944 | Q   | Ward Hall            | 1926      | Y | Consolidated     | 1926-1962 |
|    | Snead                | 1942      |     | Stinson              | 1934-1936 |   | Vultee-Stinson   | 1942-1945 |
|    | McDonnell            | 1946-1962 |     | Fairchild            | 1928-1962 | Z | Pennsylvania Airc. | 1933-1934 |
| HP | Handley Page         | 1922      |     | Bristol Aeronautical | 1941-1943 |   |                  |           |
| J  | Berliner-Joyce       | 1929-1935 | R   | Ford                 | 1927-1932 |   |                  |           |
|    | General Aviation     | 1935      |     | Maxson-Brewster      | 1939-1940 |   |                  |           |
|    | North American       | 1937-1962 |     | Ryan                 | 1941-1946 |   |                  |           |
| JL | Junkers-Larson       | 1922      |     | Aeronca              | 1942      |   |                  |           |
| K  | JV Martin            | 1922-1924 |     | American             | 1942      |   |                  |           |
|    | Keystone             | 1927-1930 |     | Brunswick            | 1942-1943 |   |                  |           |
|    | Kreider-Reisner      | 1935-1936 |     | Interstate           | 1942-1962 |   |                  |           |
|    | Kinner               | 1935-1936 |     | Radioplane           | 1943-1962 |   |                  |           |
|    | Fairchild            | 1937-1942 | RO  | Meridionali-Romeo    | 1933      |   |                  |           |
|    | Nash-Kelvinator      | 1942      | S   | Stout                | 1922      |   |                  |           |
|    | Kaiser-Fleetwings    | 1943-1945 |     | Sikorsky             | 1928-1962 |   |                  |           |
|    | Kaman                | 1950-1962 |     | Sterman              | 1934-1945 |   |                  |           |
| L  | LWF                  | 1922      |     | Schweizer            | 1941      |   |                  |           |
|    | Loening              | 1924-1933 |     | Supermarine          | 1943      |   |                  |           |
|    | Bell                 | 1939-1962 |     | Sperry               | 1950      |   |                  |           |
|    | Langley              | 1942-1943 | T   | Thomas-Morse         | 1922      |   |                  |           |
|    | Columbia             | 1945      |     | New Standard         | 1930-1934 |   |                  |           |
| M  | Martin               | 1922-1962 |     | Northrop             | 1933-1944 |   |                  |           |
|    | General Motors       | 1942-1945 |     | Timm                 | 1941-1943 |   |                  |           |
|    | McCulloch            | 1953-1954 |     | Taylorcraft          | 1942      |   |                  |           |
| N  | NAF                  | 1922-1945 |     | Temco                | 1956      |   |                  |           |
|    | Gyrodyne             | 1960      | U   | Vought               | 1922-1962 |   |                  |           |
| O  | Viking               | 1929-1936 | V   | Vultee               | 1941      |   |                  |           |
|    | Lockheed             | 1931-1950 |     | Lockheed-Vega        | 1942-1962 |   |                  |           |
|    | Piper                | 1960      |     | Vickers Canada       | 1943-1945 |   |                  |           |
| P  | Pitcairn             | 1931-1932 | VK  | Vickers              | 1922      |   |                  |           |

# SPECIAL PURPOSE SUFFIX

| | | | | |
|---|---|---|---|---|
| A | Amphibious, Armament (on normally unarmed aircraft), Arrester-gear (on non-carried aircraft), USAAF contract, Land-based version of carrier aircraft. | N | Night fighter, All-weather radar | |
| | | NA | Night fighter modified for day attack | |
| | | NL | Night fighter modified for cold-weather operations | |
| | | P | Photographic | |
| B | British contracts (Lend-Lease), Special armament, Miscellanous modification. | Q | Electronic countermeasures | |
| | | R | Transport conversion | |
| C | Cannon-armed, Stressed for catapulting, Arrested gear added. | S | Anti-Submarine (killer) | 1951-1962 |
| | | T | Trainer version | 1934-1946 |
| CP | Photographic survey (Trimtrogen camera) | U | Utility version | 1939-1962 |
| D | Drone director, Drop tanks | W | Anti-Submarine (hunter), Early Warning | |
| E | Electronic equipment | Z | Staff transport | |
| F | Flagship, re-engined version | | | |
| G | USCG version, Gunned version (on unarmed aircraft) | | | |
| H | Hospital (Ambulance) | | | |
| J | Cold-weather equipment | | | |
| K | Drone conversion | | | |
| KD | Radio-controlled drone | | | |
| L | Winterised, Searchlight carrier | | | |
| M | Missile launcher | | | |

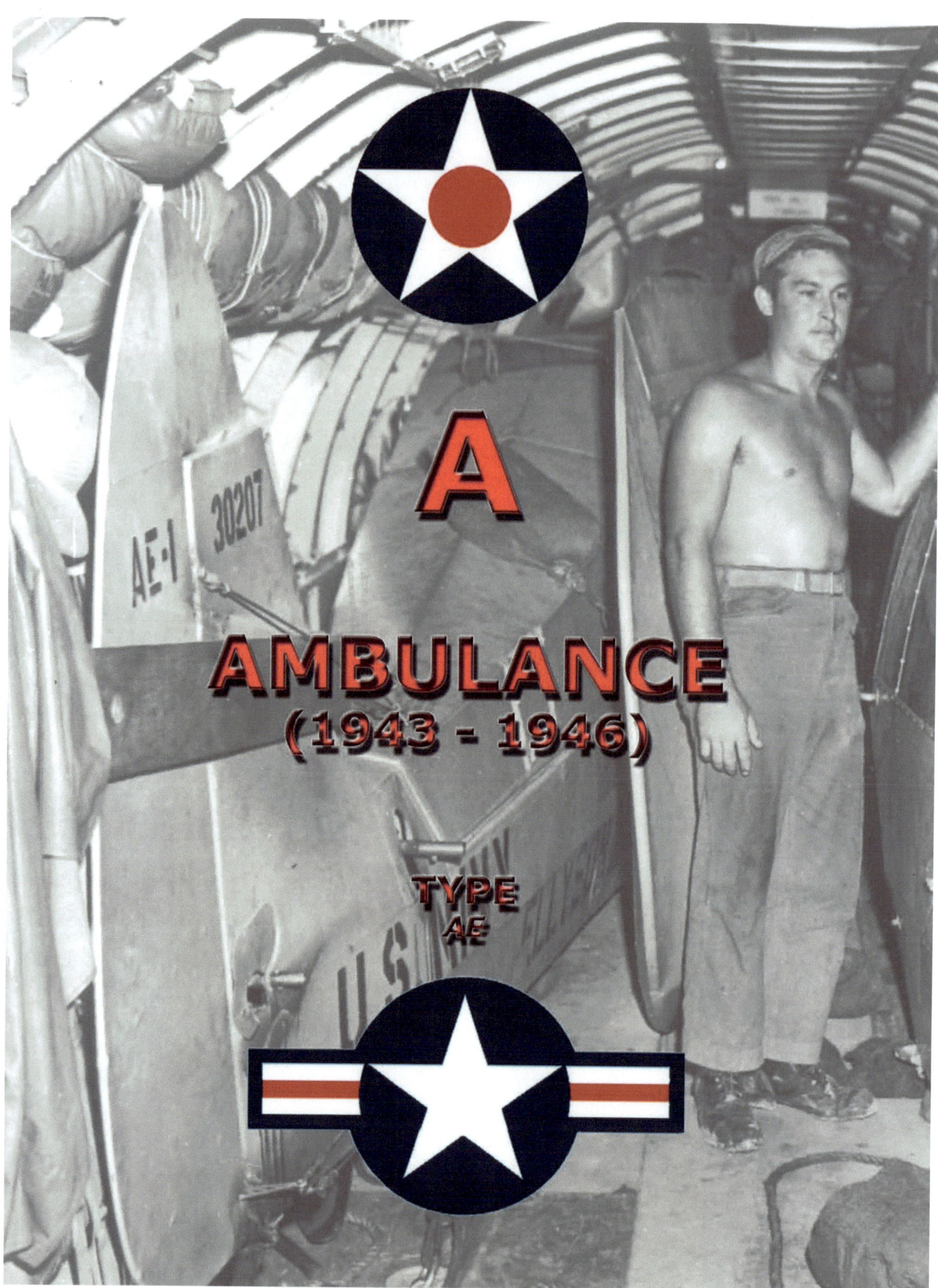

# AE-1

## Cub

**A**: Ambulance, **E**: First Piper type, **1**: Initial model

Piper first ambulance type, initial model.

| | |
|---|---|
| **Number of aircraft ordered:** | 100 |
| **Number of aircraft accepted:** | 100 |
| **Delivery dates:** | Nov.42 - Jul.43 |
| **Last stricken date:** | Feb.48 |

**Bu.No:**
**30197/30296** (100)

The AE-1 was based on the Piper J-5C which appeared in November 1941. In May 1942 one experimental J-5C was built as a two litter ambulance, with stretchers arranged one above the other. It received the Piper designation J-5CA and the registration of NX41551. The tests were successful and the US Navy decided to order the Piper J-5 ambulance, albeit with one stretcher only, with the top decking of the rear fuselage being removable to enable a single patient on a stretcher to be carried. These aircraft were designated HE-1. The first aircraft was first flown on 28 July 1942 and officially delivered to the USN on 30 November. However when in 1943, the denomination 'H' was chosen for helicopters, the surviving HE-1s became AE-1s during the first weeks of 1944.

The HE/AE-1 served mainly in the Pacific area where the evacuation of wounded soldiers was difficult and the AEs were usually stationed at small, remote air stations including in the US.

About 75% of the fleet survived the war and the survivors were soon declared as being surplus and sold on the civil market, definitively replaced by the more promising helicopter in the ambulance role.

Side view of 30288 somewhere in the States. Accepted in July 1943 it was stricken from USN inventory list on 30.11.46.

Left: Side view of 30288 with the top decking open, while 30236 is pictured from behind in the same position. 30236 was accepted in March 1943 and didn't survive the war, being lost in February 1944 but 30288 survived and was stricken on 30.11.46.

The AE was small enough to be embarked into a R5C. In those two photographs, we can see the main stages of the process. The wings were the first to be handled, then the fuselage. 30289 was accepted in July 1943 and was lost on 31.05.45 while serving with a USMC unit in the Carolines. Note the unusual markings which include the US Stars. The Piper was painted in yellow with the Red cross.

Above: Another interesting photo showing how an AE could be transported inside an R4D - possibly. Here the fuselage has been cut in half contrary to the previous photos where the fuselage was put into the R5C in one piece. 30207 was one first AE to be delivered (as an HE) in November 1942. It survived the war and was stricken from USN inventory list on 31.12.46.

Below, 30229 was accepted on 22.01.43 and survived the war too. It is seen here after the war, all yellow-painted waiting for disposal somewhere in the US. It was stricken on 31.08.46.

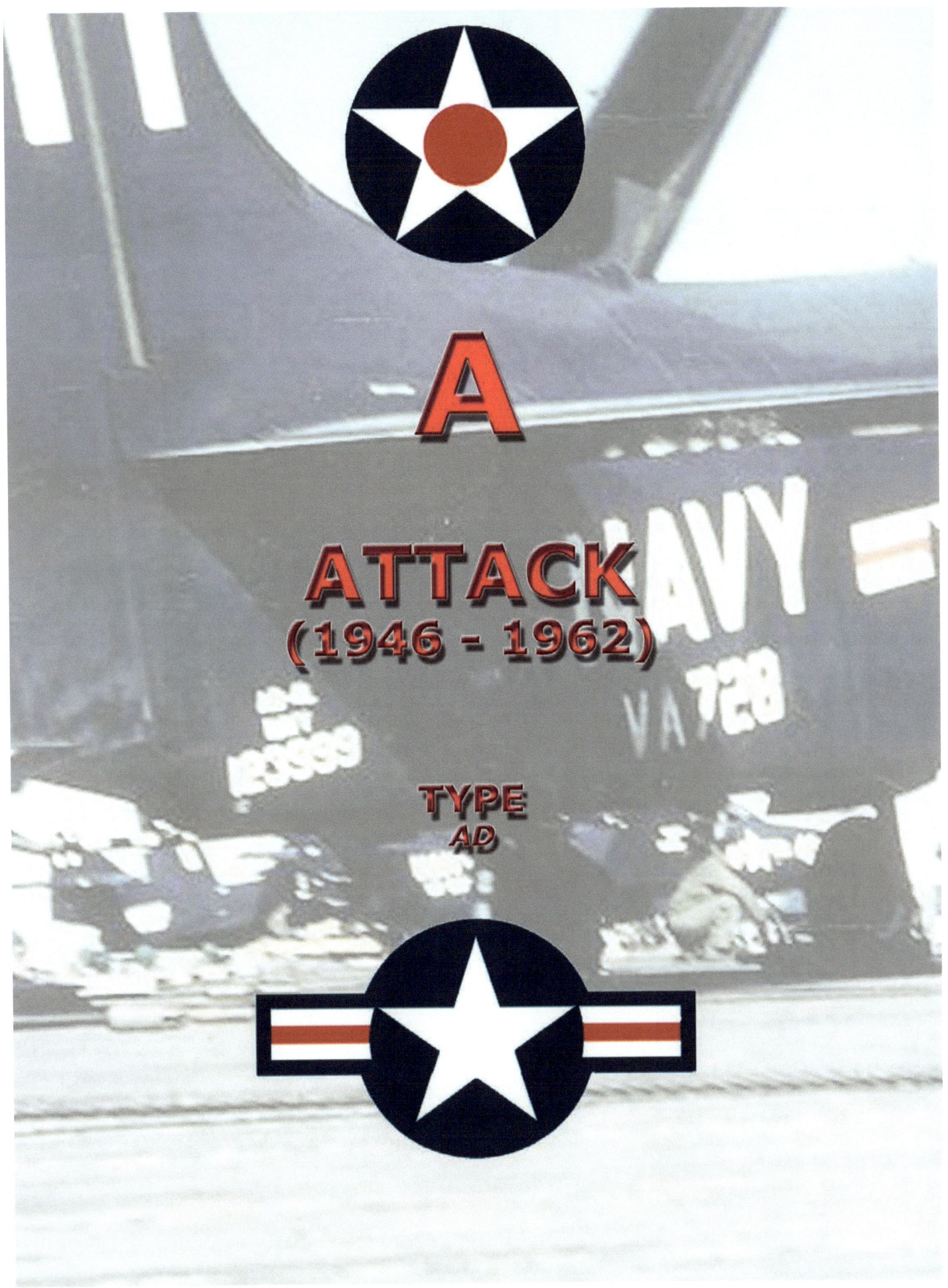

# AD-1

### *Skyraider*

**A**: Attack, **D**: First Douglas type, **1**: Initial model
Douglas first attack type, initial model.

| | |
|---|---|
| **Number of aircraft ordered:** | 242 |
| **Number of aircraft accepted:** | 241 |
| **Delivery dates:** | Nov.46 - Jan.48 |
| **Last stricken date:** | Oct.57 |

**Bu.No:**
**09110/09194** (85), **09196/09351** (156)

The AD-1 was originally ordered as the BT2D-1 in May 1945, but the denomination was changed to AD-1 when the USN refreshed its designation system in April 1946. By that time the original order had been reduced to 242 from 643. Broadly, only slight changes were introduced from the prototype, but the AD-1 had its structure strengthened which led to an increase in the empty weight. Of the 242 ordered, 241 were delivered, the last (09195) being completed as the pilot aircraft for the AD-2. Deliveries ended with the last six being accepted by the Navy in January 1948, after 10 had been accepted in 1946 and 225 in 1947. This model should be seen as an interim variant, and, even though it served as the main equipment of various first-line units, the bulk served as an advanced trainer for the type pending delivery of later versions. One of the causes of this was the continued structural failure which plagued the AD-1 during its first years.

The first USN unit to receive the AD-1 was Attack Squadron VA-19A (later re-designated VA-194) of the Pacific Fleet, soon followed by two squadrons of the Atlantic Fleet, VA-3B (later VA-44) and VA-4B (later VA-45). Other squadrons were later re-equipped totally or partially with the AD-1 including two USMC squadrons (VMA-211 and VMA-251) but by 1950, first-line units had relinquished their AD-1s for subsequent models and thus the AD-1 did not participate to the Korean War. The rest of the fleet soldiered on as trainers for a couple of years before being gradually phased out. By mid-1955 the main AD-1 user was ATU-301 and the bulk of 70 AD-1s remaining active on the Navy list were in storage, and were gradually stricken from the inventory list, the last removed on 30 October 1957. Nevertheless, the AD-1 was intensively used, with over 330,000 hours logged over almost a decade of use.

Only two derivative versions based on the AD-1 were built, the **AD-1Q** and **XAD-1W**, and in all 276 AD-1s of all versions were built.

09138 seen while taxying in 1948. This AD-1 was serving at that time with VA-3B and was wrecked in an accident in September 1953.

Top left:
09142 taken at NAS Glenview in 1949. It belongs to VA-44 (CVG-4). It was later passed on to ATU-5 with which it was wrecked in an accident in August 1950.

Middle left, believed to be 09171 flying without any ordonance. It belongs to VA-44 of CVG-4.

Below, 3/4 front view of 09199 with wings folded. It belongs to VA-2A (CVG-19). The VA-20A used the AD-1 between May 1947 and August 1948.

AD-1 09283 of VA-6B on the deck of the carrier USS *Coral Sea* (CVB 43). It was retired in September 1955 and finally stricken in February 1957 with 2,571 hours. Below, other AD-1 Skyraiders of VA-6B being spotted for launch by a plane director on board the carrier *Coral Sea* (CVB 43). VA-6B became VA-65 on 27 July 1948. With continious teething problem, the AD-1 was soon relagated to a traning role and not embarked anymore.

Above: Five AD-1s of VA-44 flying in formation formely VA-3B. The VA-44 was deployed in the Mediterranean twice in 1949 and 1950. Below, side view of 09333 of VA-55. It was retired in August 1955 and stricken in February 1957 with 2,228 flight hours.

Nice shot of AD-1 09204 of VA-20A - CVG-19. It was retired in August 1955 and stricken in February 1957 with 2,233 hours. VA-20A became VA-195 in January 1949.

# AD-1Q

## *Skyraider*

**A**: Attack, **D**: First Douglas type, **1**: Initial model, **Q**: Electronic Countermeasures
Douglas first attack type, initial model, electronic countermeasures version.

**Number of aircraft ordered:** 35
**Number of aircraft accepted:** 35
**Delivery dates:** May.47 - Jun.48
**Last stricken date:** Jun.57

**Bu.No:**
**09352/09386** (35)

The AD-1Q was based on the XBT2D-1 (09109), which was converted by Douglas as a prototype for a two-seat electronic countermeasures aircraft. Thirty-five aircraft were built, representing the balance of the original order for 277 BT2D-1 aircraft. The ECM operator's station was located within the fuselage, and radar and window (chaff) dispenser pods were attached beneath the wings, to port and starboard respectively. The first five were delivered in May and June 1947, but deliveries were stopped and were resumed about a year later. The AD-1Q retained the complete attack capabilities of the AD-1.

The first unit to be equipped with this model was VC-4 of the Atlantic Fleet, initially with 12 aircraft assigned, but by May 1950 the AD-1Q had been assigned to new Composite squadrons, VC-33 and VC-35. This was for a short time, however, as both relinquished their AD-1Qs during 1952. The AD-1Q was deployed over Korea. By 1954, 27 were still in USN hands, and were progressively withdrawn from use in the following months. They were totally obsolete by the mid-1950s, and were stricken one by one from the inventory list, the last being removed in June 1957. In all the AD-1Qs flew over 46,000 hours in USN markings.

AD-1Q 09386, the last AD-1Q built seen while being with the VC-35. Accepted on 30.06.48, it was retired in September 1954 and eventually stricken in February 1957. Of the eight AD-1Qs lost, three were wrecked during their service with VC-35, all in 1951.

Above:
Side view of 09354 before its delivery to the USN. It is still wearing the former BuNo markings on the tail. It was accepted on 16.06.47 and was retired in January 1957 only and stricken the same month.
Below:
Side view of 09372 prior to delivery to the USN in May 1948. The AD-1Q retained its full attack capabilities including the underwing and fuselage stations and the 20mm cannons. 09372 was one of the last to be stricken in June 1957 with 2,315.0 flight hours.

# XAD-1W

## *Skyraider*

**X**: Experimental, **A**: Attack, **D**: First Douglas type, **1**: First model, **W**: Airborne Early warning

Douglas first attack type, initial model, experimental airborne early warning version.

**Number of aircraft ordered:** 1
**Number of aircraft accepted:** 1
**Delivery dates:** Nov.47
**Last stricken date:** Mar.53

**Bu.No:**
**09107** (1)

One of the 25 XBT2D-1s ordered, 09107, was actually delivered as an XAD-1W, a prototype for a three-seat airborne early warning version. Two radar operators were accommodated aft of the pilot and a large opaque fairing extended behind the pilot's canopy. No armament was carried. This experiment was conclusive as it led to the production of over 400 airborne early warning ADs, the AD-3W, AD-4W and AD-5W.

The XAD-1W was eventually struck off charge on 1 March 1953 with 523.0 hours logged.

The XAD-1W taken in flight around NAS Patuxent River while carrying out tests at the NATC.

# AD-2

## *Skyraider*

**A**: Attack, **D**: First Douglas type, **2**: Second model
Douglas first attack type, second model.

**Number of aircraft ordered:** 157
**Number of aircraft accepted:** 157
**Delivery dates:** Apr.48 - Nov.48
**Last stricken date:** Jul.57

**Bu.No:**
**09195** (1), **122210/122365** (156)

Douglas modified AD-1 09195 as a pilot aircraft for the AD-2 series which had wheel-well covers, revised cockpit internal arrangement, an increase in internal fuel capacity from 365 US gallons (1,382 l) to 380 US gallons (1,438 l) and greater structural strength. The latter improvement resolved the main problem which affected the AD-1. The engine was now the more powerful R-3350-26W.
Soon after the AD-2 had joined the fleet in 1948, war in Korea broke out, and the AD-2 was intensively used by the Navy (in units such as VA-702 and VF-194) and the Marines (VMA-121) during the three years the conflict lasted. About one third of all AD-2s were lost in the Korean area of operations. Because of this, and with the introduction of new models, the AD-2 was progressively withdrawn from front-line units and served for the next few years in various second-line units, mostly in advanced training. By 1957, 45 were still held in storage facilities but all were eventually stricken and scrapped in the following weeks. Over 187,000 hours were flown on AD-2s.
The AD-2 had only two derived variants, the **AD-2Q** and **AD-2QU**, though one further unofficial designation is known to have been applied, the AD-2D applied to two AD-2s used as drones to sample radioactive materials during nuclear tests. In all, 179 AD-2s of all versions were built.

122323 of VF-54 seen in flight during the Koeran War. It survived and was later stricken in February 1957 with 1,524 flight hours.

Top:
An unidentified AD-2 of VA-2B from CVB-41 (USS *Midway*) on the ground at Naval Auxilliary Air Station (NAAS) Saufley at the end of the forties.

Middle:
After the Koeran war, many AD-2s found their way in training units, like 122214, here belonging to ATU-301. They were often flying alongside other models like AD-4 seen behind - 128982. 122314 was stricken in February 1957.

Bottom, an unidentified AD-2 belonging to VA-702 flying over the Koeran countryside. The VA-702 lost seven AD-2s in the area in 1951.

# AD-2Q

## *Skyraider*

**A**: Attack, **D**: First Douglas type, **2**: Second model, **Q**: Electronic Countermeasures
Douglas first attack type, second model, Electronic countermeasures version.

| | |
|---|---|
| **Number of aircraft ordered:** | 22 |
| **Number of aircraft accepted:** | 21 |
| **Delivery dates:** | Sep.48 - Apr.49 |
| **Last stricken date:** | Feb.57 |

**Bu.No:**
122366 - 122372 (7)/122374 - 122387 (14)

A two-seat version of the AD-2, the AD-2Q, was ordered and the aircraft were delivered between September 1948 and February 1949. (One modified machine, 122373 was accepted slightly later, in April 1949).
The other AD-2Qs served in various VC units and were engaged in Korea. By mid-1955, only nine aircraft were still flying. In the next few months they were eventually withdrawn from use and all were stricken by February 1957. In all over 23,000 flying hours were flown by the AD-2Q fleet over an eight year period.

122385 seen early in its career with VA-65. 122385 was finally stricken in February 1957 with 1,659 flight hours.

The first and the last built but two different fates!
Above, 122366 of VC-33 accepted on 10.09.48 was quickly lost in January 1952. Below, 122386, the last AD-2Q seen here serving in Korea with the VMC-1. It was eventually stricken in February 1957 with 2,276 flight hours.

# AD-2QU

## Skyraider

**A**: Attack, **D**: First Douglas type, **2**: Second model, **Q**: Electronic Countermeasures, **U**: Target-towing
Douglas first attack type, second model, target-towing version based on a electronic countermeasures version.

| | |
|---|---|
| **Number of aircraft ordered:** | **1** |
| **Number of aircraft accepted:** | **1** |
| **Delivery dates:** | **Apr.49** |
| **Last stricken date:** | **Feb.57** |

**Bu.No:**
**122373** (1)

One AD-2Q, 122373 was modified to serve in the target-towing role. If 122373 ever carried the denomination AD-2QU, this was not reported on its movement card. After conclusive trials, it was used by VU-3 and retired in June 1955 before being stricken from the inventory in February 1957.

The sole AD-2QU, 122373. The denomination under the tail is clearly readable under the tail but the its card doesn't report a such denomination.

# AD-3

## Skyraider
**A**: Attack, **D**: First Douglas type, **3**: Third model
Douglas first attack type, third model

**Number of aircraft ordered:** 125
**Number of aircraft accepted:** 124
**Delivery dates:** Nov.48 - Jul.49
**Last stricken date:** Sep.57

**Bu.No:**
122729/122852 (124)

Initially, the denomination AD-3 was reserved for a project which gave rise to the XA2D-1. With this change, this denomination was retained for an improved version of the AD-2. The AD-3 introduced an improved undercarriage with longer stroke, a redesigned cockpit canopy, an improved propeller and engine cooling system, and further local structural strengthening. All but 16 were delivered in 1949.
The AD-3 was intensively used in Korea, and among the main users in the conflict were VMA-121 and the VA-923. Around 30 were lost in the Korean zone of operations and after the war, the AD-3 was progressively relegated to other roles, including as a trainer, for example with CQTU-4. By the beginning of 1955, only 50 were still in use, and the number decreased rapidly during the year. With over 158,000 hours flown, the AD-3s were finally retired and stricken from the inventory in 1956-57. Various versions were built from the AD-3, including the **AD-3E**, **AD-3N**, **AD-3Q**, **AD-3S** and **AD-3W** totalling 193 aircraft.

The first AD-3 122729 during a test flight before being acccepted by the Navy. It was lost in Korea in August 1952 while being with the VMA-121.

Above, another loss of the Korean war, 122753. Accepted in January 1949, it is here seen while serving VF-194. It was sent to Korea with VA-923 with which it was lost in October 1951.
Left a line-up of VF-194 AD-3s with 122753 in the forefront. Behind it, 122731 which was later passed on to VC-11 and wrecked in May 1952.
Below, 122766 was luckier and survived to be stricken in November 1956 with 2,119 flight hours.

Above, AD-3 122743 of VMA-121 with its full load of ordonance ready for another strike in Korea. 122743 survived the war but was later wrecked in July 1955 still serving VMA-121.
Below, leading the formation, AD-3 122748 of VC-35 a short time before it was lost in May 1952.

# AD-3E

## *Skyraider*

**A**: Attack, **D**: First Douglas type, **3**: Third model, **E**: Electronic equiped
Douglas first attack type, third model, electronic equiped version.

**Number of aircraft ordered:** 2
**Number of aircraft accepted:** 2
**Delivery dates:** Aug.49 - Sep.50
**Last stricken date:** Nov.53

**Bu.No:**
**122906/122907** (2)

The last two AD-3W aircraft ordered were diverted from the production line for modification to AD-3E standard, to demonstrate the feasibility of using the Skyraider in a 'hunter-killer' team for anti-submarine warfare. The AD-3E was intended to work with the AD-3S in this role. The proposal was not approved in that form, and instead, specific equipment was retrofitted to existing AD-3W aircraft to carry out the AD-3E's tasks.
Both AD-3Es were used by VX-1 (Experimental Squadron One), where one, 122906, was lost in an accident on 2 January 1952 when returning from a visual cross country training flight. The pilot encountered an electrical fire in the cockpit and was obliged to make an emergency landing at Boca Chica, fortunately without injury. The remaining AD-3E, 122907, was used until August 1953 when it was withdrawn and eventually stricken from the inventory in November 1953. Indeed, at that time, there was little need to convert it to AD-3W configuration as the USN already had the AD-4W in service. The two AD-3E aircraft flew 1,900 hours with VX-1.

Side view of AD-3E 122906 in flight before it was wrecked in an accident in January 1952.

# AD-3N

## *Skyraider*

**A**: Attack, **D**: First Douglas type, **3**: Third model, **N**: Night attack
Douglas first attack type, third model, night attack version.

**Number of aircraft ordered:** 15
**Number of aircraft accepted:** 13
**Delivery dates:** Sep.49 - May.50
**Last stricken date:** Jul.57

**Bu.No:**
**122908/122922** (13)

Of the 194 AD-3 aircraft ordered in the batch 122729-122922, the last 15 were eventually ordered as a three-seat night attack version; all but one were delivered in 1949. Before completion, the last two of the initial order were actually built and accepted as the AD-3E variant.
The AD-3N served mainly with two Composite units, VC-33 and VC-35. After the Korean War, and with the widespread adoption of the AD-4 and subsequent versions, the AD-3N was progressively withdrawn from use and stored. The 13 AD-3Ns logged close to 17,500 hours during their service for the Navy.

Side view of AD-3N 122922, the last built and accepted in October 1949. It was stricken five years later.

# AD-3Q

*Skyraider*

**A**: Attack, **D**: First Douglas type, **3**: Third model, **Q**: Electronic countermeasures
Douglas first attack type, third model, electronic countermeasures version.

| | |
|---|---|
| **Number of aircraft ordered:** | 23 |
| **Number of aircraft accepted:** | 23 |
| **Delivery dates:** | Jun.49 - Feb.50 |
| **Last stricken date:** | Mar.57 |

**Bu.No:**
122854/122876 (23)

In the batch of AD-3s ordered by the US Navy, 23 were planned to be delivered as AD-3QU target tugs. However the need for such a version disappeared and all were delivered as AD-3Q aircraft, all but one handed over in 1949. The AD-3Q could be quickly adapted to use the Mk.22 aerial target system, hence the cancellation of the AD-3QU version.
The AD-3Q aircraft were generally used by Composite squadrons (VC), including some service in Korea. After the Korean War, 14 AD-3Qs continued to serve with VCs for a while but were soon replaced by the AD-4Q. The last AD-3Q was stricken from the inventory in March 1957. A total of 27,000 hours were flown by this version.

The first AD-3Q taken at Douglas facility shortly before to be handed over to the Navy in June 1949. It was wrecked in a flying accident in August 1955 while flying for VC-33.

# AD-3S

## *Skyraider*
**A**: Attack, **D**: First Douglas type, **3**: Third model, **S**: Anti-submarine - killer
Douglas first attack type, third model, anti-submarine (killer) version.

| | |
|---|---|
| **Number of aircraft ordered:** | 2 |
| **Number of aircraft accepted:** | 2 |
| **Delivery dates:** | Nov.49 |
| **Last stricken date:** | n/a |

**Bu.No:**
**122910/122911** (2)

Two AD-3 aircraft were diverted from the AD-3N contract and delivered to the USN as AD-3S aircraft, to accompany the AD-3E in their anti-submarine mission. Both were accepted in November 1949. They were tested at VX-1 (Experimental Squadron One), but the concept was not adopted by the USN, the mission-specific equipment later being installed in the existing fleet of AD-3N aircraft. Neither survived long - 122911 was lost with its crew of three on 3 April 1951 during a search run off Boca Chica, while 122910 was lost three weeks later during a torpedo tracking flight when it was forced to ditch, causing no major injuries to the crew. Both aircraft flew close to 1,300 hours with VX-1.

AD-3S 122910 seen in flight before it ditched off Boca Chica on 25.04.51.

# AD-3W

## *Skyraider*

**A**: Attack, **D**: First Douglas type, **3**: Third model, **W**: Airborne Early Warning
Douglas first attack type, third model, airborne early warning version.

**Number of aircraft ordered:** 31
**Number of aircraft accepted:** 29
**Delivery dates:** Jun.49 - Aug.50
**Last stricken date:** Dec.56

**Bu.No:**
**122877/122905** (29)

The AD-3W was the first production model of the three-seat airborne early warning configuration tested on the single XAD-1W. The crew consisted of one pilot and two radar operators.
This version had a large belly mounted radome housing a search radar. All but two were delivered in 1949 and the last two of the original order were built as AD-3Es. The AD-3Ws mainly served with VC-11 and VC-12, and saw service during the Korean War, but were rapidly replaced by the AD-4W and the AD-5W. By 1955, the USN still had 20 AD-3W aircraft on the books but they were soon retired and eventually stricken from the inventory list in December 1956. Nearly 30,000 flight hours were logged by this version.

Left, the first AD-3W, 122877 showing its right side. Accepted in June 1949 it was stricken in May 1956 with over 630 flight hours logged.

Below, 122880 taken during a test flight before its delivery to the USN. It was stricken in December 1956 with 1,201 flight hours.

# AD-4

## Skyraider
**A**: Attack, **D**: First Douglas type, **4**: Fourh model
Douglas first attack type, fourth model.

**Number of aircraft ordered:** 374
**Number of aircraft accepted:** 285
**Delivery dates:** Jul.49 - Feb.52
**Last stricken date:** Nov.59

**Bu.No:**
**122853** (1), **123771/123951** (181), *124007/124036 (30) - canx*, **127844** (1), **127853/127855** (3) **127860/127865** (6), **127867** (1**)**, **127873/127879** (7), **128917/128936** (20), **128944/128970** (27), **128979/129016** (38)

The AD-4 was built in larger number than any other aircraft in the Skyraider series, being produced in eight different versions over 1,051 aircraft officially built. The last AD-3 ordered, BuNo 122853, was kept by Douglas and was converted into an AD-4 which was fitted with an improved version of the R-3350, the 'dash 26-WA', and furthermore had an improved windscreen, a P-1 automatic pilot and a modified arrestor hook. The last example built received an additional 20mm cannon in each wing panel at the factory, a modification which was retrofitted in most of the existing AD-4s. Many AD-4s ordered were built under a role-specific designation (see below) while a handful were later converted to either AD-4B or AD-4L specification. The AD-4 was intensively used in Korea, but with the introduction of the latest Skyraider versions, the AD-4 was progressively withdrawn from use and by July 1958, only a handful were still in the USN inventory. Over 327,000 hours were flown on AD-4s for all sub-types.

The French purchased a number of AD-4 aircraft of all models which had been retired and stored, to replace their ageing P-47 Thunderbolts during the colonial war in Algeria. Only 20 of the 30 AD-4s purchased were actually used, the balance being used to serve as for spare parts for the French AD-4 fleet. The following AD-4s are known to have been bought:
128848, 123851, 123871, **123789**, **123797**, 123800, 123801, **123814**, **123821**, **123828**, 132831, **128832**, **128833**, **123837**, 123846, 123854, 123858, 123872, **123884**, **123895**, **123899**, **123920**, **123950**, **127865**, **128932**, 128945, **127966**, **127968**, **129001**, 129016 (total 30). Aircraft shown in bold are those which were known to be refurbished and put into French service. (see also AD-4NA)

Take off from USS *Philippines Sea* of 123851 of Attack Squadron Sixty-Five (VA-65). This Skyraider was later sold to France for its parts.

Above, 123900 of the Fleet Air Gunnery Unit (FAGU). It was later passed on to VMA-251 with which it was wrecked in June 1955.

Left, 128935 seen in January 1954 after its mishrap while with VMA-211. It wasn't repaired and was stricken soon after.

Below, AD-4 128920 painted with white and red paints of ATU-301 during the late fifties. It was stricken in November 1959 only with 2,631 flight hours. Behind an AD-4B, 128942 which knew a long career as well, until October 1958.

Above, AD-4 123855 of Attack Squadron VA-55 on deck landing. It was lost in Korea in June 1951.

Below, 123846 while serving with the French Air Force (EAA 1/21) based at Jibouti. Most of AD-4s were among the last ones to be refurbished and then knew a short career with the French. This AD-4 is still using the former codes of the squadron1/20 from which it received the flying equipment when formed in October 1963. it was later changed to 21-LW in December 1963. It was lost in a flying accident in April 1965, one of the two AD-4s lost by accident. Of the 113 Skyraiders put into French service (AD-4 and AD-4NA), 34 were wrecked between 1960 and 1972. (*via J-L Gaynecoetche*)

# AD-4B

## *Skyraider*

**A**: Attack, **D**: First Douglas type, **4**: Fourth model, **B**: Special armament
Douglas first attack type, fourth model, special armament version.

| | |
|---|---|
| **Number of aircraft ordered:** | 193 |
| **Number of aircraft accepted:** | 193 |
| **Delivery dates:** | Nov.51 - Jun.53 |
| **Last stricken date:** | Jan.60 |

**Bu.No:**
127854/127860 (7), 127866 (1), 127868/127872 (5), 128937/128973 (7)
128971/128978 (7), 132227/132391 (165)

The AD-4B was built to deliver nuclear weapons by using the toss-bombing, over-the-shoulder technique. As a result, this version was specially strengthened and had a special centerline ejector rack. It was also armed with four wing-mounted 20mm cannon.
The first AD-4Bs were diverted from an AD-4 contract, and only aircraft of the last batch of 165 were ordered as AD-4Bs. They were used by USN and USMC Attack squadrons. When the Navy began to introduce more sophisticated aircraft able to carry an atomic bomb, the AD-4B became obsolete and was retired. It was however used by various second-line units until the end of the 1950s. Attrition was high, with over 70 aircraft lost to all causes over a seven year period, in over 248,000 hours flown by the version.

Accepted in January 1953, 132275 ended its career with the Navy Reserve at Grosse Ile (MI). As the majority of the surviving AD-4Bs, it was stricken from the Navy List on 15.07.58.

Above, 132305 of VF-54 in flight. It was stricken in October 1958 with 2,777 hours logged.

Left, 127866 is one of the first AD-4B to have been accepted by the Navy. It is seen here serving Fleet Aircraft Service Squadron 11 (FASRON 11).

Below, Left, 127858 - here with the Attack Squadron Sixty-Five (VA-65) - is one of the first AD-4B to have been accepted by the Navy. It was also stricken in October 1958.

# AD-4L

## *Skyraider*

**A**: Attack, **D**: First Douglas type, **4**: Fourth model, **L**: Winterised
Douglas first attack type, fourth model, winterised version.

| | |
|---|---|
| **Number of aircraft ordered:** | 99 |
| **Number of aircraft accepted:** | 99 |
| **Delivery dates:** | Dec.50 - Oct.51 |
| **Last stricken date:** | Dec.58 |

**Bu.No:**
**123935** (1), **123952/124005** (54), **127725/127760** (36), **127845/127852** (8)

To respond to the need for carrying out missions during the harsh winters in Korea, AD-4 123935 was modified in February 1951 with anti-icing and de-icing equipment. The conversion was successful and 98 other AD-4s were built, diverted from existing AD-4 contracts. At the same time, two more 20mm cannon were installed.
The AD-4L was intensively used in Korea by the Navy and USMC and was essential during winter time, with around a dozen lost to all causes during the conflict. After the Korean War the need for such a specialised version decreased and many were relegated to training roles. By 1956 fewer than 50 AD-4Ls were still in the USN inventory, and the bulk of these were stricken in July 1957, with the very last ones removed in 1958. Nevertheless, the AD-4L fleet flew close to 105,000 hours.

AD-4L 123999 seen during a cruise with Attack Squadron Seven Hundred Twenty-Eight (VA-728) off the Korean coasts. It was later passed on to VA-55 and was wrecked in an accident in May 1953.

# AD-4N

## *Skyraider*

**A**: Attack, **D**: First Douglas type, **4**: Fourth mode, **N**: Night attack
Douglas first attack type, fourth model, night attack version.

| | |
|---|---|
| **Number of aircraft ordered:** | 307 |
| **Number of aircraft accepted:** | 171 |
| **Delivery dates:** | Feb.50 - May.54 |
| **Last stricken date:** | Mar.57 |

**Bu.No:**
**124128/124156** (29), **125707/125741** (35), **126884/126902** (19), **126926/126946** (21), **126970/126987** (18), **127011/127018** (8), **127880/127920** (41)

The AD-4N was the three-seat attack version of the AD-4. While 307 were ordered, only 171 were delivered as AD-4Ns, the others being accepted as either as AD-4NA or AD-4NL models.
On their acceptance by the Navy, they were rushed into service in Korea where they were intensively used by two Composite squadrons, VC-33 and VC-35. The Marines used a handful of AD-4Ns in their Composite squadrons as well.
Once the Korean War ended, the survivors were progressively converted into AD-4NA aircraft, and, by early 1956, 123 AD-4Ns had become AD-4NAs. It seems that only Bu.No 124148 remained in AD-4N specification before being retired in August 1956. It was stricken from the inventory the following March with 1822 hours to its airframe.

AD-4N 124150 seen while serving with Experimental Squadron One (VX-1). Accepted in August 1950, it was later converted to an AD-4NA in September 1955 and ended its career at the NAATC (Naval Air Advanced Training Command) in May 1957 after having flown close to 1,900 hours.

Above, AD-4N 125716 early in its career with VMC-1 (Marine Composite Squadron One) before it was converted to an AD-4NA in August 1954. It was eventually sold to France in 1960 and later handed over to Chad in 1977, a rather long career indeed!
Below, accepted as an AD-4N in October 1952, 126984 was converted to an AD-4NA in September 1955 before to be lost in accident in November 1956 while serving at NATTC (Naval Air Advanced Training Command).

# AD-4NA

*Skyraider*

**A**: Attack, **D**: First Douglas type, **4**: Fourth model, **N**: Night attack version, **A**: Modified for day attack purposes
Douglas first attack type, fourth model, night attack version modified for day attack missions.

**Number of aircraft ordered:** 100
**Number of aircraft accepted:** 100
**Delivery dates:** Jun.52 - Oct.52
**Last stricken date:** Mar.59

**Bu.No:**
**125742/125764** (23), **126876/126883** (8), **126903/126925** (23), **126947/126969** (23),
**126988/127010** (23)

The AD-4NA was an AD4-N stripped of its night attack equipment, and thus was only able to carry out strikes during daytime. The type was used intensively in Korea. Only 100 aircraft were ordered as AD-4NAs, but many were built from AD-4N contracts and many conversions (at least 119) from the latter version took place after the end of the Korean War. This type was progressively replaced by subsequent types and by mid-1958, after having logged over 302,000 hours (AD-4N & NA) with US forces, all but a handful of these aircraft had been retired. At that time most were waiting to be scrapped when the French expressed an interest in purchasing those of them still in good condition. The AD-4Ns purchased by France were then re-accepted by the USN for a short time for administrative purpose. The designation **A-1D** was earmarked in September 1962, but was never taken up even by the French (see also AD-4).

Only 93 of the 117 AD-4NAs purchased were actually used, the balance serving to provide spare parts for the French AD-4 fleet. The following AD-4NAs are known to have been purchased:
**124134, 124140, 124140, 124142, 124143, 124146,** 124155, **124156, 125714, 125715, 125716, 125717,** 125718, **125719, 125721, 125722,** 125723, **125724, 125728,** 125730, **125732, 125734, 125735, 125740, 125741, 125744, 125746, 125749, 125755, 125762, 126877, 126878, 126880, 126882, 126888, 126890, 126893, 126894, 126897,** 126899, **126900, 126901, 126903, 126910 - 126914,** 126918, **126920 - 126924, 126927, 126929, 126931, 126933 - 126935, 126938, 126940, 126942, 126945, 126949, 126952,** 126953, **126954 - 126960,** 126961, **126962, 126964 - 126966,** 126967, **126969, 126970, 126973,** 126976, **126979,** 126981, **126983,** 126985, **126986,** 126988, **126994 - 126998, 127002, 127004,** 127009, **127012,** 127014, 127016, **127881,** 127884, **127888, 127893 - 127895,** 127897, 127899, **127900,** 127901, **127903,** 127905, 127906, 127908, 127911, **127919**. Those aircraft which were actually refurbished and put into active service are shown in bold. The entire French Skyraider fleet flew over 107,000 hours between 1960 and 1977 and were used by six squadrons. Surplus aircraft were later handed over to Cambodia, Chad and Gabon.

AD-4NA 125762 seen in flight while serving with the VF-194 in Korea. It survived the war and was later sold to France. It eventually ended its career in Cambodia, being amongs the machines handed over by the French in the mid-sixties.

Above, another AD-4NA sold to France, 126920, here seen serving at the Naval Air Reserve Unit - NARU - at Atlanta (GA). It was later declared surplus with the French in May 1964 when they decided to reduce their Skyraider fleet.
Right, 126957 was also sold to France after having served at NARU Glenview (IL) and met the same fate in Fance in 1964.
Below, 124134 while serving at the FAETULANT (Fleet Airborne Electronics Training Unit Atlantic). This Skyraider was accepted as an AD-4N in April 1950 and converted in July 1954 before to be withdrawn from use in July 1956 with 2,210 hours flown. It was of the first AD-4NA sold to France and served until crashing to destruction in August 1971.

Above, AD-4NA 126930 was accepted as an AD-4N but converted to an AD-4NA in June 1954. It was one of the very last AD-4NA to be stricken from inventory in March 1959.
Below, two AD-4NAs of Attack Squadron Eight Hundred Twenty-Two (VA-822) flying from Naval Air Reserve Unit, Louisiana. 126986 was accepted as an AD-4N and was later sold to France with which it served until May 1964 while 127002 was accepted as an AD-4NA. It was also later sold to France with which it served until to withdrawn from use in August 1976.

Top, 125711 seen while serving at Miramar (CA). This aircraft had a short career with the Navy, 26 months, being withdrawn from use in September 1956 and stricken two years later.

Center, 125741 while serving in a reserve unit at Grosee Ile (MI). Accepted as an AD-4N in June 1952, it was converted to an AD-4NA in April 1956. It was stricken from inventory in July 1958 as many of its type and was later sold to France. It served until being wrecked in a crash on 06.06.72.

The bulk of the French Skyraiders were AD-4NA like 127919, seen serving with the squadron 2/20 *'Ouarsenis'*. It was the penultimate AD-4NA built but the last accepted by the Navy. In French service it was withdrawn from use in May 1964.
(via J-L Gaynecoetche)

Above, AD-4NA 125732 of the E.C. 1/20 'Aurès-Némentcha' seen in flight. It was destroyed in an accident on 11.06.63.
(via J-L Gaynecoetche)

Left, In 1976, France handed over five AD-4NAs for usage by the Guards' squad of the Gabonese President Omar Bongo. 126956 was one of them.
(via J-L Gaynecoetche)

Below,
A Chadian AD-4NA - 126959. Seven AD-4NAs were supplied by the French from April 1976 onwards, 126959 being one of the first four. The pilots were usually French flying under a private contract and they were used against rebels in the North of the country. On 16.04.78, 126949 was shot down by an SA-7, being the last ever Skyraider lost in combat. The AD-4 were officially withdrawn from use in 1982.
(via J-L Gaynecoetche)

# AD-4NL

### Skyraider

**A**: Attack, **D**: First Douglas type, **4**: Fourth model, **N**: Night Attack version, **L**: Winterised
Douglas first attack type, fourth model, winterised Night Attack version.

**Number of aircraft ordered:** 37
**Number of aircraft accepted:** 37
**Delivery dates:** Feb.51 - Feb.52
**Last stricken date:** Mar.58

**Bu.No:**
**124153** (1), **124725/124760** (36)

In February 1951, Douglas modified one AD-4NA (124153) with the same anti-icing and de-icing equipment used on the AD-4L. Consequently, Douglas received an order for 36 AD-4NLs which were accepted between June and December 1951. The first production aircraft, 124725, was retained for a short time by Douglas, before being handed over to the USN in February 1952. Most were used in Korea over the next two years, mainly by Composite squadrons of the Navy (VC-33 & VC-35) or of the Marines (VMC-1).
When the Korean War ended in July 1953, 29 AD-4NLs were still active with the USN/USMC Squadrons. They were, however, soon withdrawn from first-line units and found a second career in reserve units, especially where its de-icing or anti-icing equipment could be useful. After a couple of years of service they were all retired and stricken with around 40,000 hours flown in total.

Only the units located in the north part of the States were interested in getting some AD-4NL. Left and below, two AD-4NLs serving with the Reserve at Grosse Ile (MI). Left, the first AD-4NL 124153, modified from an AD-4N. It was stricken in June 1957 with 2,228 hours to its airframe. Below 124748 of the now named Naval Air Reserve Unit (NARU) wearing the new tail codes for Grosse Ile '7Y' introduced in June 1952 and the Orange fuselage band. 124748 was stricken in May 1957 after having flown 1,322 hours. It had previously served with VC-35 (see next page).

Before serving at Grosse II with the NARU, 124748 served with Composite Squadron Thirty-Five (VC-35) here seen in flight over the sea.

# AD-4Q

## *Skyraider*

**A**: Attack, **D**: First Douglas type, **4**: Fourth model, **Q**: Electronic Countermeasures
Douglas first attack type, fourth model, electronic countermeasures version.

| | |
|---|---|
| **Number of aircraft ordered:** | 39 |
| **Number of aircraft accepted:** | 39 |
| **Delivery dates:** | Nov.49 - Sep.50 |
| **Last stricken date:** | May.59 |

**Bu.No:**
124037/124075 (39)

The need of an aircraft able to carry out electronic countermeasures missions led to the production of the AD-4Q, a two-seat aircraft. This version served mainly in various VC squadrons - VC-33 being the main user - which included action in Korea. Attrition was high and by 1955 only 17 remained in service so replacement was required. The introduction of the AD-5Q allowed the surviving AD-4Q aircraft to be phased out in 1957 after having logged 41,000 hours.

Left, 124061 embarked on the USS *Forrestal* in 1955 which had just been commissioned. 124061 was among the last AD-4Q to be stricken, in June 1958 with 2,610 hours logged.

Below, The first AD-4Q - 124037 - but accepted by the Navy in April 1950 only. It was retired in December 1956 with 1,117 flight hours and was stricken in July 1957.

# AD-4W

## Skyraider

**A**: Attack, **D**: First Douglas type, **4**: Second model, **W**: Airborne Early Warning
Douglas first attack type, fourth model, airborne early Warning version.

**Number of aircraft ordered:** 148 (+20 MDAP)
**Number of aircraft accepted:** 148
**Delivery dates:** Mar.50 - Nov.52
**Last stricken date:** Dec.56

**Bu.No:**
**124076/124127** (52), **124761/124777** (17), **125765/125782** (18), **126836/126875** (40), **127921/127961** (41 - last 20 MDAP)

The AD-4W was a three-seat airborne early warning version of the AD-4 of which 168 were eventually built, including 20 for the British under the Mutual Defense Assistance Program (MDAP). As for the USN aircraft, the last of 148 ordered was accepted in November 1952. They were used by composite squadrons (mainly VC-11 & VC-12) and by August 1956 the type had been retired after having logged over 121,500 hours in US markings, and the fleet stricken in December.

The British were looking for an airborne early warning aircraft to be embarked in their aircraft carriers. Having no British aircraft yet available, the Americans agreed to supplied the AD-4W to fulfil the role. The British Royal Navy was supplied with 50 aircraft, 20 of which were newly built by Douglas, the remaining being refurbished former USN aircraft. They were delivered by batches starting in November 1951 and became Skyraider AEW.1s in UK service. For operational use, only one Fleet Air Arm unit, 849 Squadron, was formed, the squadron being established in 1952. It was divided into five flights, each having four Skyraiders apiece, which were distributed among Royal Navy aircraft carriers at sea. The last Skyraider AEW.1 aircraft were delivered in November 1955. The AD-4Ws supplied were 124080, 124085, 124086, 124097, 124101, 124103, 124104, 124107, 124110 - 124116, 124121, 124122, 124761, 124765, 124768, 124771, 124774, 124777, 126846, 126849, 126866, 126867, 127922, 127942 - 127961.

Two AD-4Ws of the Composite Squadron Thirty-Five (VC-35) during the Korean War. Left, 124771 which was later handed over to the British FAA as WT967 and below 124115 which was also saw later service with the British but as WV179.

Top: AD-4W 126840 with special electronics gear carries a crew of three consisting of a pilot and two interceptor operators. It belongs to Marine Composite Squadron One (VMC-1) during the Korean War. Accepted in June 1952 it was withdrawn from use in August 1956 and stricken from inventory in December the same year with 471 flight hours.

In the middle, another AD-4W of VMC-1, 124772 which was accepted in May 1952. It was withdrawn from use in May 1955 and stricken from inventory with 901 flight hours in April 1956.

Left: The British FAA was the only user abroad with 50 machines taken on charge and they were used by a single operational unit, No.849 Sqn with various detachments. In front WV103, formely 124085 which had been accepted in May 1950 before to handed over to the British in September 1952. The type was withdrawn from use in 1960. Eight was wrecked in various accident while serving the Royal Navy.
They were originally allocated the following serials: **WT943-WT949, WT982-WT987, WV102-WV109** and **WV177-185**; however serials were incorrectly applied to five as **WT097, WT112, WT121, WT761** and **WT849**.

# AD-5

## Skyraider

**A**: Attack, **D**: First Douglas type, **5**: Fifth model
Douglas first attack type, fifth model.

**Number of aircraft ordered:** 213
**Number of aircraft accepted:** 213
**Delivery dates:** Nov.51 - Sep.54
**Last stricken date:** *post Sept.62*

**Bu.No:**
**124006** (1), **132392/132476** (85), **132478** (1), **132637/132686** (50), **133854/133929** (76)
*132687/132728 (42) canx, 133930/134004 (75) canx, 134076/134233 (176) canx*

The AD-5 was the most radical revision of the airframe, being turned into a two-seat attack bomber with the crew sitting side by side. The forward section of the fuselage was heavily redesigned, as were the vertical tail surfaces which were increased in area by nearly 50%. A centerline pylon was also added.
First flown on 17 August 1951 (BuNo 124006), this model led to the production of three other versions, the AD-5N, AD-5Q and AD-5W, giving a total of 669 AD-5s built. They were used by both the Navy and the Marines and by September 1962, 140 AD-5s were re-designated **A-1E**.

AD-5 132458 of Marine Attack Squadron Three Hundred Thirty-One (VMA-331) on the ground showing the new silhouette introduced with this variant. 132458 never became an A-1E being lost in July 1957 while serving with VFA(W)-4.

49

Above, AD-5 133893 of Naval Air Reserve Training Unity (NARTU) Los Alamitos flying over southern California before it was denominated A-1E. Left, 132466 of Attack Squadron Forty-Five (VA-45). 132466 was later on denominated A-1E, something which never happened to 133875, below, seen here while flying with Marine Attack Squadron Three Hundred Thirty-One (VMA-331) on the ground at Bishop Airport, Flint, MI. It was wrecked in a flying accident in November 1959.

Above, AD-5 133882 of Marine Aircraft Repair Squadron Twenty-Seven (MARS-27) on the ground at Marine Corps Air Station (MCAS) Cherry Point. This Skyraider was later passed on to the USAF and was lost in Vietnam in April 1966.

Below, 132447 of Marine Aircraft Engineering Squadron Twelve (AES-12) based at Quantico. As for 133882 it was passed on the USAF and was lost in Vietnam only six weeks after the latter.

Above, AD-5 132396 while with Attack Squadron Ninety-Five (VA-95) at the end of the fifties. This squadron used the Skyraider for two deployments aboard the USS *Ranger* (CVG-9 - tail code NG). This specific aircraft was lost in an accident in March 1960.

Sometimes denominated AD-5U, it seems that this denomniation remained unoffcial however as this AD-5 133878 of Utility Squadron One (VU-1) was still carrying the denomination 'AD-5' when this photo was taken. This AD-5 was later converted back to combat configuration and served in Vietnam with both USAF and VNAF.

Two other AD-5s of Naval Air Reserve Training Unit (NARTU), 133881 and 133905. Of the two, only 133905 became an A-1E, 133881 being lost in April 1961.

# AD-5N

## *Skyraider*

**A**: Attack, **D**: First Douglas type, **5**: Fifth model, **N**: Night attack
Douglas first attack type, fifth model, night attack version.

**Number of aircraft ordered:** 323
**Number of aircraft accepted:** 239
**Delivery dates:** Jan.53 - Jun.55
**Last stricken date:** *post Sept.62*

**Bu.No:**
**132477** (1), **132480/132636** (157), **134974/135054** (81), *135055/135138 (84) - canx*

The AD-5N was the night attack version of the AD-5, fitted with radar and searchlight in pods beneath the wings. They mainly served with VC-33 and VC-35, later with VA(AW)-33 & 35.
They were re-designated **A-1G** in September 1962, though this applied to only 94 AD-5Ns, partly because of attrition, but also because 54 AD-5Ns were converted to AD-5Q status from 1958 onwards.

AD-5N 132498 of VA(AW)-35 which became an A-1G in 1962.

Top, 132562 seen before the introduction of the new camouflage sheme in 1955. It was serving Composite Squadron Thirty-Three (VC-33) when the photo was taken. It was accepted in August 1954 and later on, it was passed on to the USAF and was lost in Vietnam on 05.09.65.

Middle left, 132605 at Grosse Ile Naval Reserve Station, MI. It later became an A-1G.

Below, 132553 of Marine Composite Reconnaissance Squadron Three (VMCJ-3) which also became an A-1G.

Above, two AD-5N flying in formation, 132591 and 135051 while flying for VAW-13. Both became an A-1G in 1962.

Left, 134994 of VA(AW)-35 embarked on the USS *Bonhomme Richard*. This one became an A-1G as well.

Below, one of the first AD-5N, 132481 seen while serving Naval Air Reserve Unity (NARU) Minneapolis at Naval Air Facility (NAF) Litchfield Park. Navy and Marine are both painted on the side. This Skyraider became an A-1G later on.

# AD-5Q

## *Skyraider*

**A**: Attack, **D**: First Douglas type, **5**: Fifth model, **Q**: Electronic countermeasures

Douglas first attack type, fifth model, electronic countermeasures version.

| | |
|---|---|
| **Number of aircraft ordered:** | 54 (conversion) |
| **Number of aircraft accepted:** | 54 |
| **Delivery dates:** | 1957 - 1958 |
| **Last stricken date:** | *post Sept.62* |

**Bu.No:**
Known numbers: 132506, 132513, 132529, 132532, 132534, 132543, 132545, 132549, 132555, 132567, 132572, 132575, 132576, 132578, 132580, 132581, 132589, 132590, 132591, 132594, 132599, 132603, 132611, 132613, 132621, 134974, 134982, 134983, 134984, 134985, 134988, 134992, 134993, 134994, 134995, 135009, 135010, 135018, 135028, 135029, 135031, 135034, 135044, 135048, 135049, 135051, 135054.

The AD-5Q was a version resulting from conversion kits fitted to AD-5Ns and never produced as new. The last AD-5N, BuNo 135054 was converted to carry out electronic countermeasures work. Once tests were completed, more kits were produced and 53 AD-5Ns were converted in 1957-1958. In September 1962, 42 were still in the USN inventory and they were re-designated **EA-1F**.

> Three AD-5Qs of VA(AW)-33 flying in formation. If 132590 and 132575 were re-designated EA-1F after September 1962, 135995 was wrecked in an accident in a couple of weeks before, in June 1962, still flying with VA(AW)-33.

# AD-5S

## Skyraider

**A**: Attack, **D**: First Douglas type, **5**: Fifth model, **S**: Anti-Submarine - killer
Douglas first attack type, fifth model, anti-Submarine (killer) version.

| | |
|---|---|
| **Number of aircraft ordered:** | 1 |
| **Number of aircraft accepted:** | 1 |
| **Delivery dates:** | May.53 |
| **Last stricken date:** | n/a |

**Bu.No:**
**132479** (1)

One experimental ASW aircraft fitted with MAD (Magnetic Anomaly Detector) was tested by VX-1 at Key West, Florida. The tests carried out did not give rise to any production orders and the sole AD-5S was converted to AD-5N standard in July 1956.

The unique AD-5S seen while serving with the VX-1 (tail codes 'XA'). Behind, AD-4N 124150 used by the VX-1 at the same time for various tests.

# AD-5W

## Skyraider

**A**: Attack, **D**: First Douglas type, **5**: Fifth model, **W**: Early Warning
Douglas first attack type, fifth model, early warning version.

**Number of aircraft ordered:** 252
**Number of aircraft accepted:** 218
**Delivery dates:** Jun.53 - Mar.56
**Last stricken date:** post Sep.62

**Bu.No:**
132729/132792 (64), 133757/133776 (20), 135139/135222 (84), 138535/138568 (34) canx,
139556/139605 (50)

The AD-5W was a four-seat airborne early warning version of the AD-5. The aircraft carried a large radome beneath the fuselage and was fitted with a new metal rear canopy.
Two main units were equipped with this version, VC-11 and VC-12 which later became VAW-11 and VAW-12 by the time the new system was introduced. At the same time, the 145 AD-5Ws which were still listed in the USN inventory became **EA-1E** aircraft under the new system.

Left, 135194 early in its career while with VMC-2. Later on, it was handed over to the VAW-12 with which it was wrecked in an accident in October 1959.
Below, 133764 was lost much more earlier in November 1956 while serving with VC-12 after 17 months of service only.

Left and below, 132789 and 135191 with the older blue paint. 135191 was accepted in June 1955 and later passed on to VAW-12 with which it was wrecked in March 1960. It is seen prior to the delivery to the VMC-2. But 132789, seen here early of its career werving with the VC-12 (later VAW-12) went through the new system.

Above: 135183 of VAW-12 (CVG-2) flying over the sea in the beginning of the sixties, while below 132751 of VAW-11 ready to be launched from the USS *Kearsage*. The tail code 'RR' was assigned to the VAW-11. Both received the new denomination EA-1E in 1962 but it is not the case for 135168 which was wrecked in August 1961 while flying with VAW-11.

# AD-6

## *Skyraider*

**A**: Attack, **D**: First Douglas type, **6**: Sixth model
Douglas first attack type, sixth model.

**Number of aircraft ordered:** 713
**Number of aircraft accepted:** 713
**Delivery dates:** Jun.53 - Aug.56
**Last stricken date:** *post Sep.62*

**Bu.No:**
**134466/134637** (172), **135223/135406** (184), **137492/137632** (141)
**139606/139821** (216)

The AD-6 was basically an improved AD-4B fitted with special equipment for low-level attack bombing, and bomb racks of improved type first used on the AD-5. They were produced concurrently with the two-seat AD-5. The AD-6 remained the most-produced single model of the Skyraider (not counting models with sub-types), with 713 built. The AD-6 was powered by an R-3350-26WA instead of the 26W of the AD-5.
With the introduction of the A4D Skyhawk from the late 1950s onwards, the number of AD-6 aircraft began to decrease rapidly, and by 1960 only 14 Attack squadrons were still active on Skyraiders. By that time, many had been put into storage or stricken from the inventory, and the model had even begun to be supplied to the Vietnamese Air Force (VNAF). That is why in 1962, only 368 AD-6s remained to be denominated **A-1H** following the introduction of the Tri-service system.

AD-6 139621 of Attack Squadron 122 had the task to provide trained pilot for Skyraider units. 139621 is one 368 AD-6s to have received the denomination of A-1H in 1962.

Above 135349 of Attack Squadron 15 (VA-15). It was accepted on 02.09.54 and was wrecked in April 1957 while serving Marine Attack Squadron 324 (VMA-324).

Left another AD-6 of VA-15 in flight, 134545 which was also lost while serving VMA-324 (in August 1958).

Below left, 135252 in blue while flying with Attack Squadron 195 (VA-195). It was later lost in an accident in March 1958 while flying with the VA-15.

Above, 135251 of Attack Squadron One Hundred Fifteen (VA-115) flying at sea level. The VA-115 was one of the seven Skyraider squadrons of the Pacific Fleet in 1960, while Attack Squadron One Hundred Ninety-Six (VA-196), left, was one of the seven squadrons of the Atlantic fleet with VA-176 (below). 135284 was stricken from inventory in October 1960, while 135251 became an A-1H, and 135536 ended its career with the VNAF.

135308 of VA-196 wearing the older identification letter of ATG-1 'U' which was changed to 'NA' on 30.09.58. 135308 is another AD-6 which later served with the VNAF.

Attack Squadron 145 (VA-145) was one of the seven Skyraider squadrons in January 1960. 137628 was later transferred to the USAF and was eventually lost in Vietnam on 09.04.71.

Attack squadron 165 (VA-165) was commissioned on 01.09.60 on Skyraiders at NAS Jacksonville and saw active service in Vietnam on that type. 139609 became an A-1H after 1962.

Left, AD-6 139665 of VA-122. When the the new Tri-service sytem was introduced, the VA-122 was providing training for Skyraider pilots for the fleet, a role it kept until 1967. 139665 was later passed on to the VNAF and was one of the 11 Skyraiders to escape to Thailand in April 1975.

Above, AD-6 135399 of VMA-324 before the squadron transitioned to the A4D-2.

Bottom, line-up of AD-6s of Fighter Squadron Fifty-Four (VF-54) on the ground a Naval Air Station (NAS) Alameda.

Above, two AD-6s of VT-30s which became the source of Skyraider pilots for the front-line units from July 1960. 135279 was later passed on to the VNAF. Below, 134605 of VA-152 one of seven squadrons of the Pacific Fleet still flying the Skyraider in 1962. The VA-152 deployed over Vietnam with Skyraiders a couple of years later. This AD-6 was later passed on to the VNAF as well.

Above, two AD-6s of Marine Attack Squadron Three Hundred Thirty-One (VMA-331), a couple of months after having been reestablished. Its home at the end of the 50s was Opa Locka in Florida. The VMA-331 did a single deployment around that date while flying the AD-6. Soon after it converted to the A4D-2 Skyhawk in 1958-1959.
Below, one of the first Skyraider received by the VNAF in 1960. They were still AD-6s and they arrived on 24 September 1960. Here 134473 is in service with 1st FS, which was later became 514th FS in 1963. The AD-6 (A-1H) will become the bulk of the Vietnamese Skyraider fleet in the followings years to come and they served until the fall of Saigon in April 1975.

The penultimate AD-6, 139820 while serving with Attack Squadron One Hundred Forty-Five (VA-145) of the Pacific Fleet. It also became an A-1H in September 1962

# AD-7

## Skyraider

**A**: Attack, **D**: First Douglas type, **7**: Seventh model
Douglas first attack type, seventh model.

| | |
|---|---|
| **Number of aircraft ordered:** | **240** |
| **Number of aircraft accepted:** | **72** |
| **Delivery dates:** | **Aug.56 - Feb.57** |
| **Last stricken date:** | **post Sep.62** |

**Bu.No:**
**142010/142081** (72), 142546/142626 (84) - canx, 143050/143133 (84) - canx

The AD-7 was the last production version of the Skyraider. It differed from the AD-6 in being powered by an R-3350-26WB instead of an R-3350-26WA and in having a strengthened undercarriage, engine mountings and outer wing panels.
The Navy had first planned to order 240 of these, but the last two batches were later cancelled in favor of jet-powered A4Ds, the AD being by then seen as at its end of the service life. The 72 AD-7s ordered were initially delivered to three VA squadrons, but it became soon clear that the AD-6 and AD-7 were very similar, giving no significant problems regarding maintenance, and both types were eventually used by VA squadrons at the same time without segregation.
When the Tri-service system was introduced, 46 AD-7s remained in the USN inventory and they were designated **A-1J**. At that time, 14 front-line VA squadrons were still equipped with ADs, seven in the Pacific fleet and seven in the Atlantic fleet, the AD-7 being part of the equipment of most of them.

Left, 142010, the first AD-7 built. It was issued to VA-95, one of the first squadrons to operate the Dash 7. It carries the codes of Carrier Air Group Nine (CVG-9). This AD-7 became A-1J later on.
Below, AD-7 142020 was also assigned to VA-95 but was lost in accident in August 1960 still serving the same unit. This photo was taken prior to October 1958 when the CVG-9 was assigned the letter 'N' which was altered to 'NG' on 30.09.58.

Above, 142012 of VA-115 while part of CVG-11. AD-7 142012 was denominated A-1J and later served with VA-152 in Vietnam to be eventually posted missing in action with its pilot on 10.08.65.
Left, 142069 of the VA-54 of the CVG-5. It later served with VA-95 with which it was wrecked in accident in June 1962.
Below, 142029 of VA-216 (ATG-4). Becoming an A-1J, it was finally handed over to the USAF to serve in Vietnam and was lost in action over Laos on 26.04.69.

Another view of 142029 serving this time with VA-122 at an early stage of its career. VA-122 was part of CVG-12 at that time. It later saw service with the USAF.

www.ingramcontent.com/pod-product-compliance
Lightning Source LLC
Chambersburg PA
CBHW042009150426
43195CB00002B/71